10
ten

9
nine

8
eight

7
seven

6
six

5
five

4
four

3
three

2
two

1
one

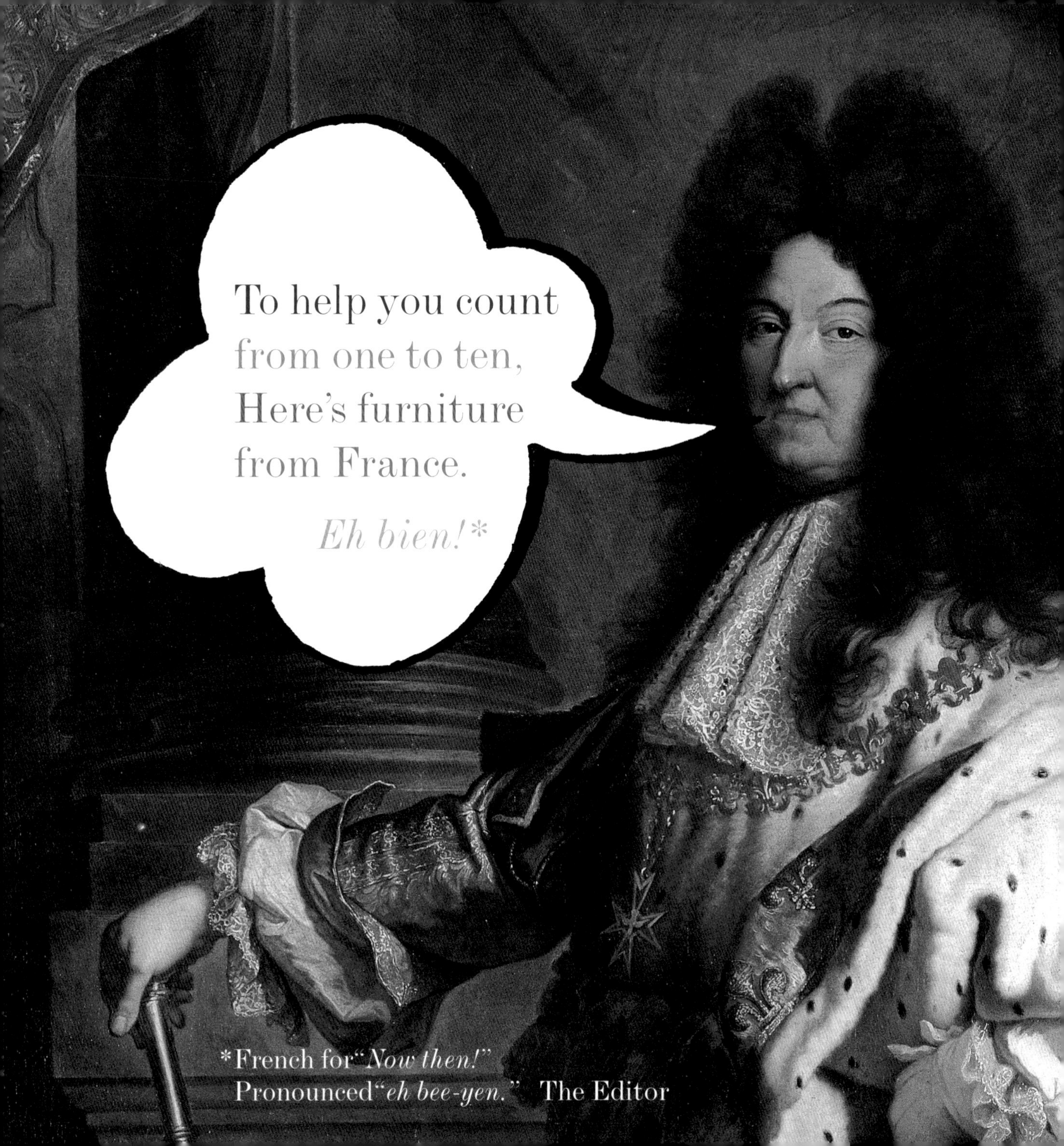

*French for "*Now then!*"
Pronounced "*eh bee-yen.*" The Editor

1 to 10

and back again

A Getty Museum Counting Book

The J. Paul Getty Museum, Los Angeles

one globe

two beds

3

three desks

four candleholders

five cabinets

6

six cups

zero saucers

seven tables

eight chairs

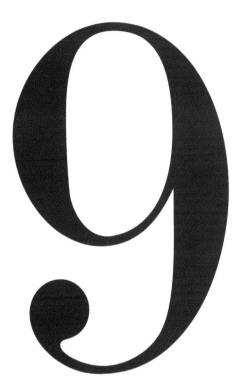

nine vases

10

ten clocks

That was easy,

n'est-ce pas?*

OK:

Now count these up.

Begin!

Commencez!**

How many chairs and how many

clocks?

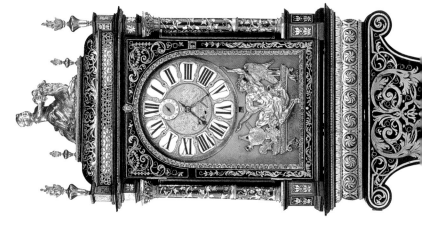

le grand total =

10

How many
and

vases

how many beds?

le grand total = **9**

How many cabinets and how

many

le grand total = 8

How many tables and how many

candleholders?

le grand total = **7**

How many globes

and

how many desks?

le grand total = 6

How many clocks

and how many

cups?

le grand total = 5

How many cabinets

and how many

candleholders?

le grand total = 4

How many chairs

and how many

globes?

le grand total = 3

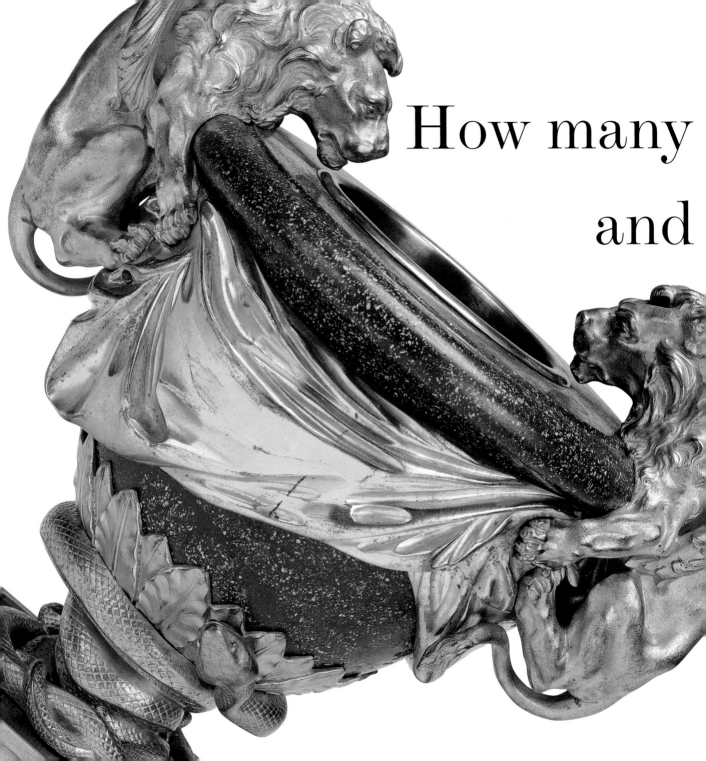

How many

and

vases

how many tables?

le grand total = 2

How many
beds?

le grand total = 1

Les Objets*

*You know what this means. Pronounced *"layz aub-zhay."* The Editor

1 *Side chair* 1780–81   2 *Tripod table* about 1680   3 *Cabinet* about 1745   4 *Cup* 1759   5 Cup 1770   6 *Covered cup* about 1760   7 *Cup* 1773
8 *Wall clock* about 1740   9 *Armchair* about 1730   10 *Mantel clock* about 1790   11 *Candleholder* about 1745   12 *Vase* about 1745   13 *Globe* about 1728

14 *Standing vase* about 1785   15 *Corner cupboard* about 1750   16 *Vase* 1754–55   17 *Side table* about 1730   18 *Candleholder* about 1785

19 *Table* about 1680   20 *Armchair* about 1735   21 *Armchair* about 1790   22 *Rolltop desk* about 1785   23 *Model for a mantel clock* about 1700

1 *Cabinet* about 1765   2 *Mantel clock* about 1763   3 *Wall light* about 1720   4 *Vase* 1761   5 *Mantel clock* about 1720   6 *Vase* 1785   7 *Cabinet* about 1785
8 *Wall clock on a bracket* about 1764   9 *Cabinet on stand* about 1675   10 *Vase* 1768–69   11 *Mantel clock* about 1772   12 *Lidded vase* about 1768

13 *Wall clock* about 1710   14 *Long-case musical clock* about 1712   15 *Bed* about 1750   16 *Chandelier* about 1818   17 *Reading and writing table* about 1670
18 *Swivel chair* about 1787   19 *Double desk* about 1750   20 *Armchair* about 1770   21 *Writing and card table* about 1725   22 *Armchair* 1762

1 *Table* about 1770 2 *Cup* 1761 3 *Cup* 1781 4 *Bed* about 1775 5 *Table* about 1760 6 *Vase* about 1765 7 *Long-case clock* about 1680

8 *Armchair* about 1735 9 *Portrait of Louis XIV* After Hyacinthe Rigaud, 1700s 10 *Vase* about 1765 11 *Desk* about 1700

For Gillian

© 1999 The J. Paul Getty Museum
1200 Getty Center Drive, Suite 1000, Los Angeles, California 90049-1687

Christopher Hudson, Publisher
Mark Greenberg, Managing Editor

Project staff:
John Harris, Writer and Editor
Pamela Patrusky Mass, Designer
Suzanne Petralli Meilleur, Production Coordinator
Jack Ross, Photographer
Nancy Ogami, Illustrator

Printed and bound by Tien Wah Press, Singapore
Library of Congress Catalog Card Number: 98-9930
ISBN 0-89236-525-0